PEOPLE AT
THE CENTER OF

PROHIBITION

By TAMRA B. ORR

BLACKBIRCH™
PRESS

THOMSON

GALE

San Diego • Detroit • New York • San Francisco • Cleveland
New Haven, Conn. • Waterville, Maine • London • Munich

Photo credits: cover, pages 10, 11, 17, 18, © Hulton/Archive; cover, pages 5, 13, 15, 21, 22-23, 25, 37, 44-45 © CORBIS; pages 6-7, 20 © Underwood & Underwood/CORBIS; page 8 © Michael Maslan Historic Photographs/CORBIS; pages 9, 39 © Hulton-Deutsch Collection/CORBIS; page 12 © Stapleton Collection/CORBIS; pages 14, 27, 28, 29, 30, 31, 32, 33, 34, 35, 36, 38, 40, 41, 43 © Bettmann/CORBIS; page 16 © Library of Congress; page 24 © David J. & Janice L. Frent Collection/CORBIS; page 26 © National Portrait Gallery

LIBRARY OF CONGRESS CATALOGING-IN-PUBLICATION DATA

Orr, Tamra.
  Prohibition / by Tamra B. Orr.
    v. cm. — (People at the center of:)
  Includes bibliographical references and index.
  Contents: The cast for the drys — Carry Nation (1846-1911) — Chapter 3 and on the side of the wets — Al Capone (1899-1947).
    ISBN 1-56711-768-6 (hardback : alk. paper)
  1. Prohibition—United States—Juvenile literature. 2. United States—History—20th century—Juvenile literature. [1. Prohibition. 2. United States—History—1919-1933. 3. United States—Social life and customs—1918-1945.] I. Title. II. Series.

  HV5089.O67 2004
  363.4'1'0973—dc21   2003004210

Contents

PEOPLE AT THE CENTER OF

PROHIBITION

The history of alcohol in the United States predates the founding of the nation itself. American colonists of the seventeenth and eighteenth centuries drank alcoholic beverages such as beer, rum, wine, and cider because they were often safer than the impure water or unpasteurized milk available at the time. Liquor was believed to be beneficial to health, and few men and women would let a day, or in some cases, a few hours, pass without a drink. By the early 1800s, some citizens began to seriously question the wisdom of habitual drinking. Physicians and ministers feared for the health and moral behavior of people who consumed alcohol. Mothers and wives feared that their husbands would spend money on alcohol instead of food and clothing; and others believed that alcohol would eventually drive an honest, hardworking man to a life of laziness and poverty, or even worse, violence or crime. Citizens against alcohol began to preach temperance (the use of alcohol sparingly and cautiously) and gave birth to the temperance movement.

Temperance leaders believed that their message of temperance would appeal to people's sense of morality, and that Americans would eventually stop drinking alcohol voluntarily. What began as a moral crusade, however, became a political one, as laws intended to destroy the liquor trade and prohibit, or stop, people from drinking alcohol became the new focus. No one expected this to be an easy fight. The production of liquor was one of the largest industries in the country, and taxes on liquor provided enormous revenues for the government.

In the late 1800s, groups of people who wanted to fight for prohibition formed organizations. The Prohibition Party, for example, supported prohibitionist candidates for political office. In 1874, a group of Protestant women established the Women's Christian Temperance Union (WCTU), and in 1895, prohibitionists formed the Anti-Saloon League, which became a major force in American politics.

In the 1800s, temperance leaders presented the rejection of alcohol as a moral choice the individual must make, as shown in this temperance banner.

VIRTUE, LOVE & TEMPERANCE.

LOVE, PURITY & FIDELITY.

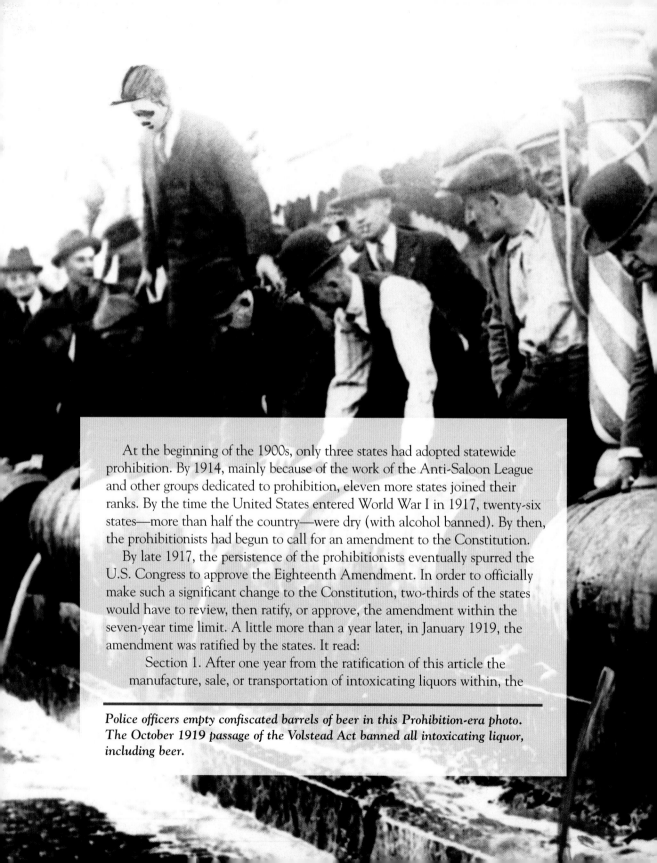

At the beginning of the 1900s, only three states had adopted statewide prohibition. By 1914, mainly because of the work of the Anti-Saloon League and other groups dedicated to prohibition, eleven more states joined their ranks. By the time the United States entered World War I in 1917, twenty-six states—more than half the country—were dry (with alcohol banned). By then, the prohibitionists had begun to call for an amendment to the Constitution.

By late 1917, the persistence of the prohibitionists eventually spurred the U.S. Congress to approve the Eighteenth Amendment. In order to officially make such a significant change to the Constitution, two-thirds of the states would have to review, then ratify, or approve, the amendment within the seven-year time limit. A little more than a year later, in January 1919, the amendment was ratified by the states. It read:

Section 1. After one year from the ratification of this article the manufacture, sale, or transportation of intoxicating liquors within, the

Police officers empty confiscated barrels of beer in this Prohibition-era photo. The October 1919 passage of the Volstead Act banned all intoxicating liquor, including beer.

Above: The Washington State Legislature (pictured) was one of the state legislatures that approved the Eighteenth Amendment. Opposite: Those who wanted to drink alcohol during Prohibition found their way to speakeasies.

importation thereof into, or the exportation thereof from the United States and all territory subject to the jurisdiction thereof for beverage purposes is hereby prohibited.

Section 2. The Congress and the several States shall have concurrent power to enforce this article by appropriate legislation.

Section 3. This article shall be inoperative unless it shall have been ratified as an amendment to the Constitution by the Legislatures of the several States, as provided in the Constitution, within seven years from the date of the submission hereof to the States by the Congress.

In October, Congress adopted the Volstead Act, or the National Prohibition Act, which provided for the enforcement of the amendment and gave federal authorities the power to prosecute violations. The act also defined intoxicating liquor as that containing 0.5 percent alcohol by volume, which, much to the surprise and disappointment of many, included beer.

Anti-Prohibition groups scrutinized the wording of the amendment to find every loophole possible. For example, Section 1 states that people are not allowed to make, sell, or transport liquor, but it does not state that it could not be bought or consumed. In response, people stockpiled alcohol in their homes before the amendment went

into effect. According to the law, if the alcohol was already on the premises, it was not illegal to drink once Prohibition began. In addition, the amendment says nothing about using alcohol for medicinal purposes. Suddenly doctors and pharmacists found themselves making a fortune by writing prescriptions for millions of gallons of liquor for those who claimed they needed it for health purposes.

Prohibition had many effects on the economy. Saloons and taverns did not go out of business. Instead, they changed into speakeasies, bars that sold illegal alcohol. Proprietors asked their customers to talk softly and keep quiet about it—hence the name. The bigger the city, the more speakeasies it had. In New York, for example, there were approximately five thousand speakeasies in 1922; four years later, there were about thirty-two thousand. Other sectors of the economy suffered because of Prohibition. When the distilleries were shut down, the demand decreased for barley and hops, two of the ingredients in beer. As a result, farmers lost enormous amounts of money.

Prohibition invited unlawful behavior. For example, some people, called rum-runners and bootleggers, illegally transported liquor from government warehouses or Canada to the bars. Others became owners of distilleries and made and sold alcohol. Another type of criminal, the gangster, sold illegal liquor, became rich, and as a result, gained power and control over parts of the larger cities. Gangsters often had their own mobs, groups of criminally minded followers with no respect for the law. Violence erupted as mobs fought each other for control of neighborhoods. Police officers and other law enforcement officials ignored the unlawfulness around them in exchange for bribes. As criminals became some of the most powerful and glamorous people in cities, and the law enforcement system grew corrupt, the American people grew skeptical of the honesty of public officials and began to lose respect for the law.

During Prohibition, people thought of ways to keep drinking without being caught.

Revelers celebrated the end of Prohibition in 1933. The Twenty-first Amendment repealed the Eighteenth Amendment and made alcohol legal again.

Although liquor consumption did decrease substantially between 1914 and 1935, it soon became obvious that people still bought, sold, and drank liquor under Prohibition. Anti-Prohibition groups pushed for a repeal of the Eighteenth Amendment. They protested that Prohibition had invaded their civil liberties and increased unlawfulness. They also argued that the legalization of liquor would bring thousands of badly needed jobs and tax revenues.

With Democrat Franklin D. Roosevelt as the nation's new president, Congress proposed the Twenty-first Amendment to repeal the Eighteenth Amendment in February 1933. Before the amendment was ratified by the states, Roosevelt sent a special message to Congress that requested the legalization of beer. The bill, which amended the Volstead Act, legalized beer of 3.2 percent alcohol content by weight. The bill passed in both houses and became effective on April 7, 1933. Hundreds of distilleries opened, and thousands of bottles of free beer were handed out in celebration. Seven months later, after enough states had voted in favor of the Twenty-first Amendment, it was officially ratified and liquor, beer, and wine were legal again. The Eighteenth Amendment became the only amendment to the Constitution ever repealed.

BENJAMIN RUSH

CLAIMED THAT LIQUOR MADE PEOPLE ILL

Benjamin Rush was born in 1746 near Philadelphia. He was only fifteen when he graduated from the College of New Jersey at Princeton and he received his doctorate in medicine from the University of Edinburgh in Scotland in 1768. Rush returned to the United States and eventually became the first professor of medicine at the University of Pennsylvania. He was also a signer of the Declaration of Independence, and named physician-general of the Continental army.

Unlike many of his colleagues, Rush did not think liquor was good for a person's health. In a pamphlet, *An Inquiry into the Effects of Ardent Spirits Upon the Human Body and Mind,* published in 1785, he wrote that over time, distilled liquors made a person physically sick and prone to fighting, swearing, and crime. He claimed that alcohol that was fermented (beer, wine, and cider) was acceptable in moderation. His pamphlet changed the way thousands of people viewed alcohol and inspired the beginning of the temperance movement.

In a later edition of his pamphlet, Rush included a "Moral and Physical Thermometer" that showed how continual drinking could eventually lead to depression, madness, jail time, and outright anarchy and hatred of the government. Rush was one of the first people to ever refer to chronic drunkenness as a disease, rather than just poor judgment. His pamphlets sold as fast as they could be printed and were in print for several decades. Rush favored temperance over prohibition and believed in educating people about the risks of alcohol consumption. He was considered the first real father of the temperance movement.

In his later years, Rush focused on the mentally ill. His work and research into this field earned him another title: "Father of American Psychiatry." He also worked for the abolition of slavery and educational rights for women. Rush died in 1813. Long after his death, his publications were still being used and quoted by temperance speakers and writers.

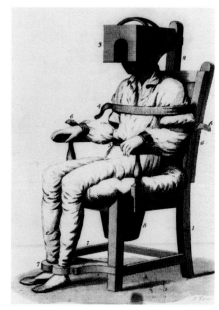

Opposite: Benjamin Rush felt chronic drunkenness was a disease. Above: In his later life, Rush researched mental illness and invented the tranquilizing chair (pictured).

Lyman Beecher was born in New Haven, Connecticut, in 1775. A graduate of Yale College, he later became a preacher and spoke out about the sinfulness of alcohol. In 1825, he delivered a series of sermons at his church and declared liquor one of the primary sources of evil in the country. The following year these sermons were published in a book titled *Six Sermons on the Nature, Occasions, Signs, Evils and Remedy of Intemperance*.

In this publication, Beecher tried to appeal to the emotions of his readers. He wanted them to see that alcohol was not just a national issue, but also a potential problem in their own homes. He preached that even drinking a little now and then was a risk because occasional drinking led to constant drinking. The only solution was to become a teetotaler, or person who abstained from any kind of alcohol, including beer and wine. The book went through several editions and became enormously popular. It was constantly quoted in newspapers and magazines and by speakers and became the basic text of the temperance movement.

Above: Teetotalers like Lyman Beecher warned that occasional drinking leads to drunkenness. Opposite: Beecher was a preacher whose collection of sermons formed the fundamental text of the temperance movement.

Beecher moved to Boston, and along with Reverend Justin Edwards, a Boston clergyman who opposed alcohol, he worked on a movement already under way to unify several of the small and scattered temperance groups into one large, national society. The organization, the American Society for the Promotion of Temperance, was established in February 1826, and within ten years had almost a million members.

The abolition of slavery was just as important to Beecher as the banning of alcohol, and his passion was passed on to his children. His son, Henry Ward Beecher, became a strong advocate for ending slavery; and his daughter, Harriet Beecher Stowe, wrote *Uncle Tom's Cabin*, a novel about the cruelty of slavery. Lyman Beecher died in 1863 at the age of eighty-eight.

Frances Elizabeth Caroline Willard was born in 1839 in Churchville, New York. She lived briefly in Ohio, then moved with her family to Wisconsin territory. In this isolated region, Frances saw no one outside of her immediate family for months at a time. After a minimal number of years of formal schooling, Willard, who always yearned for an education, began to teach. Eventually she became the president of the Evanston College for Ladies. When the college merged with Northwestern University, she became the dean of the women's college.

After several years of involvement with the Women's Christian Temperance Union (WCTU), Willard became national president in 1879. She called her position a "leader of a forlorn hope," but her leadership helped the organization become very powerful. Willard traveled between fifteen and twenty thousand miles a year for almost ten years. She introduced the WCTU into the South in the early 1880s, and a few years later to every state and territory in the West.

Willard was a teacher, writer, speaker, and leader. She breathed new life into the WCTU and formed alliances with other groups for social change, such as those who supported

Opposite: As president of the Women's Christian Temperance Union, Frances Willard led the nationwide expansion of the organization. Above: The WCTU message spread throughout the United States.

woman suffrage and better working conditions. Between conventions, she went on long lecture tours that attracted large crowds and brought the WCTU into the headlines. In 1891, she became president of the world WCTU.

Friends convinced Willard to write her life story at the age of fifty. Called *Glimpses of Fifty Years*, the book, more than seven hundred pages long, told about her life as a crusader and activist. In 1898, Willard died at the age of fifty-eight in New York City.

CARRY NATION

Carry Amelia Moore was born in Kentucky in 1846. She grew up poor and worked hard. Her brief first marriage to a man named Charles Gloyd, an alcoholic, led her to despise alcohol. She remarried, this time to David Nation, a lawyer and a minister. The Nations moved to Kansas in 1890.

Carry Nation was determined to live in an alcohol-free world. At the age of fifty-three, she joined the Women's Christian Temperance Union. In 1900, she carried out the first of many attacks that were part of her crusade against alcohol. Her method was to toss stones and rocks through the front windows of a bar. Armed with a hatchet in one hand and a Bible in the other, she would then enter the bar and destroy bottles, mirrors, and furniture. Reporters followed Nation and took photographs of her for the next day's newspapers. Ironically, the owners of the bars that she targeted appreciated the publicity—and sympathy—she brought them.

Nation was arrested thirty times between 1900 and 1910, and became a symbol of the Prohibition movement. She was sought after as a lecturer, and wrote newsletters about her life's mission. In 1910, Nation became ill, and she died in 1911 at the age of sixty-five. Her tombstone reads, "She hath done what she could." Years after Nation's death, when saloons became illegal speakeasies, many of them sold their customers a terrible-tasting cocktail that was mockingly known as the Carry Nation.

This editorial cartoon depicts temperance activist Carry Nation after she physically destroyed one of many bars.

After a first marriage to an alcoholic, Nation yearned for an alcohol-free world.
Her unorthodox methods made her a symbol of the Prohibition movement.

Wayne Wheeler was born in Brookfield, Ohio, in 1869. When he was a child, an intoxicated farmhand accidentally stabbed him in the leg with a pitchfork. From that day forward, he vowed to rid the world of alcohol. He worked his way through school and graduated from Oberlin College, then the center of the temperance movement in Ohio. When Howard Hyde Russell, the founder of the Anti-Saloon League, asked Wheeler to work for the league, he accepted.

Wheeler studied law and became the national attorney as well as organizer for the Anti-Saloon League of America. He took the idea of prohibition from a state level to a federal one, and through his work with the league was instrumental in getting the league's resolution, a prohibition amendment, introduced to Congress in 1914. Wheeler and the league then worked tirelessly to ensure that there were enough representatives in Congress to vote for the amendment. They spent

Opposite: As national attorney and organizer for the Anti-Saloon League, Wayne Wheeler (left) drafted and ensured the passage of the Volstead Act. Above: Posters like this one pleaded for federal prohibition. Wheeler helped to move the issue of prohibition from the state to the federal level.

millions of dollars on campaigns in support of Prohibition candidates, organized thousands of petitions and letters to be sent to Congress, and trained up to fifty thousand lecturers to preach the league's message.

When the Eighteenth Amendment became official, Wheeler revealed his National Prohibition Act, which outlined Prohibition enforcement laws. Later it became known as the Volstead Act, named for the committee chairman whom Wheeler

The Anti-Saloon League (pictured) spent millions of dollars to back congressional candidates who would vote for Prohibition.

persuaded to introduce the article to Congress. Wheeler included in the bill his definition of an intoxicating beverage a definition that included beer and wine.

Wheeler died in 1927. After his death and the repeal of Prohibition, the Anti-Saloon League's importance faded.

Andrew Volstead, born in 1860, was the son of Norwegian immigrants. He later became the city attorney and mayor of Granite Falls, Minnesota. In March 1903, he was elected to the U.S. House of Representatives. He was interested in the issue of civil rights and fought for federal legislation that made lynching illegal. Volstead initially had little interest in the Prohibition movement. By the time Wayne Wheeler, a leader of the Anti-Saloon League of America, had drafted enforcement laws to accompany the Eighteenth Amendment, Volstead had become concerned about alcohol consumption in the United States. Wheeler chose Volstead to take these laws, known as the National Prohibition Act, and steer them through Congress. Volstead oversaw the document until what became known as the Volstead Act passed in October 1919, despite President Woodrow Wilson's veto. Three years later, Volstead helped pass a law called the Capper-Volstead Act, which empowered farmers to market, price, and sell their products cooperatively, or together. In 1923, after he had served ten terms as a representative, Volstead returned to Minnesota to practice law. He worked as a lawyer until the day he died at age eighty-six.

Above: Americans who opposed Prohibition cast U.S. representative Andrew Volstead as the Big Bad Wolf. Opposite: Volstead introduced the National Prohibition Act, which was renamed after him, to Congress and secured its passage in 1919.

STRICTLY ENFORCED PROHIBITION

Herbert Hoover was born in Iowa in 1874. In 1895 he graduated from Stanford University with a degree in geology.

In 1928, he was elected the thirty-first president of the United States. As a Quaker, Hoover had long disliked the use of alcohol. He called Prohibition "The Noble Experiment" and did everything he could to enforce it. In a controversial decision, he more than tripled the $4.4 million per year the federal budget set aside for the enforcement of Prohibition to $13.4 million. For this money, Hoover wanted to see arrests.

More people were arrested, but Hoover's plan caused other problems. For example, Prohibition agents who usually pursued gangsters and their associates turned their attention to average citizens who committed minor infractions of Prohibition laws. Americans became angry as hundreds of them were arrested each week for violating laws they did not support. Convictions for liquor offenses grew so fast that the courts could not keep up with them. Local jails were at maximum capacity, and federal prisons were overrun. New facilities had to be built to house all of the prisoners, which cost the taxpayers money.

When he ran for reelection in 1932, Hoover refused to endorse an

Opposite: President Herbert Hoover called Prohibition "The Noble Experiment." Above: Everyday Americans railed against the Hoover administration's insistence that they be arrested for minor infractions of Prohibition laws.

outright repeal of the Eighteenth Amendment. He felt that it was his presidential duty to support the Constitution as it stood, which meant the endorsement of Prohibition. His sense of duty led to his defeat. His opponent, Franklin D. Roosevelt, had made it clear that if elected, he would repeal the Eighteenth Amendment. The people heard Roosevelt, and he won the election.

After Hoover left the White House, he wrote a number of books and articles on political issues. He died at age ninety in New York City.

Isadore Einstein was a postal clerk and Moe Smith, a cigar store owner. In 1921, they traded those professions in to become Prohibition agents in New York City.

During their five years as agents, these two men, known as Izzy and Moe, made more than four thousand arrests and confiscated more than $15 million worth of alcohol. The team would do anything it took to get the job done. They dressed like women or pretended to be street cleaners or tourists to gain entrance to speakeasies. Once inside, they would ask for a drink. If they were served, they made an arrest. Newspaper stories reported that they appeared in everything from wet swimsuits in the middle of winter to mud-covered football uniforms to accomplish their goals.

Above: Isadore "Izzy" Einstein and Moe Smith made more than four thousand arrests during their five-year career as Prohibition agents. Opposite: Izzy (left) and Moe (right) used unorthodox methods to gain entrance to speakeasies.

Bootleggers were afraid of the twosome. They never took a bribe, and no one could predict where they would show up next and what they would look like.

Other Prohibition agents disapproved of the two men for their unusual methods of gaining access to speakeasies. They felt that Izzy and Moe's antics made the job of a Prohibition agent look foolish. The public and the press, on the other hand, loved the team, which sparked jealousy among their colleagues. No other agents made as many arrests as Izzy and Moe, but despite their impressive record, they were fired in 1925.

Little is known about their lives after 1925. In 1985, *Izzy and Moe,* a film about them, was released starring Jackie Gleason and Art Carney.

PROHIBITION AGENT WHO LED THE UNTOUCHABLES

Born in Chicago in 1903 to Norwegian immigrant parents, Eliot Ness had a degree in law and a strong interest in the pursuit of criminals. As a Prohibition agent, Ness was chosen to head a special investigative unit to accumulate evidence of famed gangster Al Capone's Prohibition violations. The unit, formed in August 1929, was made up of nine other agents that Ness carefully handpicked.

Prohibition agents raided many stills that belonged to Capone, which cost the gangster a lot of money and supplies. Ness became a target for Capone, and a number of attempts were made on his life. Bombs were found in his car, and on several occasions, shots were fired at him as he entered or left his home. Capone also attempted to bribe Ness and the other agents several times. When Ness and his colleagues refused to accept money from Capone in return for ignoring his illegal activities, a newspaper column called them "untouchable." Often the bribes amounted to more than these men made in a year, and it was a true sign of the agents' integrity that they refused the money.

Opposite: Prohibition agent Eliot Ness gained fame for his integrity and leadership of the Untouchables. Above: Ness pursued Al Capone (center) until the gangster was convicted.

Ness and his agents tirelessly gathered evidence of Capone's bootlegging operations. Eventually Capone and his associates were charged with thousands of Prohibition violations, but it was the charge of tax evasion that brought a conviction against Capone. When Capone was sentenced, Ness escorted the mob boss to the train as he was sent off to prison. Ness was promoted to chief investigator of the Prohibition forces for Chicago and spent the next ten years in the pursuit of more criminals.

In 1957, Ness wrote a book about his adventures called *The Untouchables*. As Ness prepared to write his second book, however, he had a heart attack and died at the age of fifty-five. His accounts of his Prohibition days led to a television series and a blockbuster movie that made the Untouchables an enduring legend.

George Remus

George Remus was born in Germany in 1876 and came to Chicago at the age of five. At the age of twenty-four, he obtained a law degree and was the defense lawyer for a number of disreputable people. He noticed that his clients made a great deal of money through illegal alcohol sales and production, and he knew he could too. He carefully studied the Volstead Act and made a plan.

First, in 1920, he took his entire life savings and bought as many distilleries, pharmacies, and whiskey certificates as he could. He knew that under the Volstead Act, the certificates would allow him to buy alcohol and sell it for medicinal purposes. Eventually, he became the owner of the largest distillery in the country. He bottled some of his whiskey as medicine and sold it through his pharmacies, but the vast majority of it was sold to bootleggers, private clients, and speakeasies. Within three years, Remus made millions of dollars and became the wealthiest bootlegger in America.

Finally, Remus was caught and arrested in 1923. From there, his life took a downward turn. After he was sentenced to two years in the Atlanta Federal Penitentiary, his wife ran off with a former federal agent and took all his money with her. In 1927, she divorced Remus after he was released, and on their way to court to arrange the divorce settlement, he chased her down and murdered her. Remus defended himself at the murder trial, and because of friendships he had with influential people, he was acquitted on grounds of temporary insanity.

Although Remus planned to return to the business of illegal alcohol, he found that Chicago

Opposite and Above: George Remus used a loophole in the Volstead Act and became the wealthiest bootlegger in America until he was arrested in 1923.

had changed. Powerful groups of gangsters controlled the liquor trade now and he could not compete with their wealth and influence. Finally, he moved to Kentucky and lived a quiet life there. It is not known when he died.

MARY LOUISE GUINAN

MISTRESS OF CEREMONIES IN THE SPEAKEASIES

Born in Waco, Texas, in 1884, Mary Louise Cecilia Guinan began to study music when she was young and soon turned to amateur theater. As a young woman, she moved to New York City in 1906 and worked as a chorus girl. A brash blonde, she was spotted by a talent scout and taken to Hollywood where she had a few small movie roles. Eventually, her movie career ended, and she returned to New York.

Above: New York speakeasies offered high-priced drinks and spirited entertainment. Opposite: Although Prohibition agents arrested Mary Louise "Texas" Guinan many times, the speakeasy owner's powerful friends kept her out of jail.

There, Guinan became an immediate hit as a mistress of ceremonies in the speakeasies. She sang songs, told jokes, and generally kept the people happy as they bought rounds of overpriced alcohol. When she came out on stage, she would smile and give her signature greeting of, "Hello, sucker!" Her southern drawl and Texas origins resulted in her new name of "Texas" Guinan. With the support of some powerful gangsters, Guinan opened up the Texas Guinan Club.

Support from gangsters enabled Guinan to stay out of jail and in business. Every time the authorities shut her down, she opened up another club. When Guinan was arrested, she was released before she had to spend any time in jail because the police were usually well paid not to interfere. As a result, Guinan and her partners took in thousands of dollars a week.

Guinan's club was typical of the nightclubs of the twenties in New York during Prohibition. The prices were high and the entertainment boisterous. Patrons were often celebrities, members of high society, or politicians, and clubs like Guinan's became regarded as chic. Although Guinan returned to Hollywood one more time and made several more films, she never became a star. She died in 1933 at the age of forty-nine and was portrayed in a number of films after her death.

Bill McCoy was born in 1877 in Syracuse, New York. In 1900 he moved to Florida and began to build boats with his brother. The sale of their boats earned McCoy and his brother Ben all the money they needed to live, but after World War I began, the demand for pleasure boats diminished. Eager to stay on the sea, the McCoy brothers decided to go into business as transporters of illegal alcohol.

Life as a rumrunner off the Atlantic coast could make a person rich or get him killed. The Coast Guard was on constant watch for runners, as were pirates who hoped to steal the alcohol on board. From his first sale of fifteen hundred cases of whiskey taken from the Bahamas to Georgia, McCoy was able to buy the first of a fleet of rum ships. Some historians believe that the origin of the phrase, the "real McCoy," is a reference to the high quality of McCoy's liquor.

Opposite: Bill McCoy, or the King of Rum Row, transported more than 170,000 cases of liquor before the Coast Guard caught him in 1923. Above: The Coast Guard confiscated the rumrunners' cargo and held it for Prohibition agents.

In May 1921, McCoy sailed a cargo of liquor north and anchored off the Long Island, New York, coast, beyond what was then the three-mile limit of U.S. waters. Bootleggers expected his arrival and sent dozens of small boats to meet him and take aboard cases of liquor. This action established what was to become known as Rum Row.

McCoy spent the next four years sailing back and forth between Nassau in the Bahamas and Rum Row. He estimated that he transported more than 170,000 cases of liquor before the Coast Guard finally caught up with him in 1923. Known by then as the King of Rum Row, McCoy showed some resistance, but eventually surrendered. After he spent some time in jail, he lived comfortably in Florida until his death at the age of seventy-one on board his beloved ship, the *Blue Lagoon*. In time, the United States won an agreement with Britain and other nations to extend territorial waters, and consequently pushed Rum Row out twelve miles to sea. This ended the ship-to-shore bootlegging that McCoy and others like him had mastered.

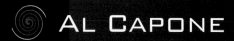
Alphonse Caponi was born in 1899 in Brooklyn, New York, to poor Italian immigrants. At the age of twenty, he moved to Chicago to work for a ruthless and prominent gangster, Johnny Torrio, eager to profit from the bootlegging racket. When Torrio retired, Capone took over his gang.

During Prohibition, Capone grew to enormous power in Chicago and became an official celebrity of the era. He mingled with politicians and business leaders, and aware of the effects of positive press, endeared himself to the American public by showy displays of charity to the poor.

In one year, Capone made $60 million from the sales of beer and liquor, $25 million from gambling, and another $20 million from other illegal businesses. The true results of Capone's activities became clearer to the public as they learned of the cold-blooded killings between Capone's gang and rival gangs and the constant use of lethal weapons on the streets. In time, Capone came to symbolize the criminal effects of Prohibition, and many people began to question the wisdom of laws that made alcohol illegal.

Although a number of attempts were made to kill Capone, they were never successful. In 1927, the FBI declared Capone as "Public Enemy Number One." When Capone finally did go to jail, it was not for the many brutal murders for which he was responsible, but for income tax evasion. He had made a great deal of money over the years and never filed or paid any taxes on it. He was sent to prison for eleven years and spent much of that time in Alcatraz, one of the toughest prisons in the country. After he was released, he had a heart attack and died in 1947 at the age of forty-eight.

Above: Mobster Johnny Torrio mentored the young Al Capone in gangland Chicago. Opposite: Capone gained wealth and power through bootlegging and became a symbol of Prohibition's underbelly.

The Association Against the Prohibition Amendment (AAPA) and other anti-Prohibition groups campaigned against the Eighteenth Amendment.

WILLIAM STAYTON

FOUGHT TO REPEAL PROHIBITION

In 1918, fifty-eight-year-old lawyer, businessman, and former navy officer, Captain William Stayton, founded the Association Against the Prohibition Amendment (AAPA). Although the amendment had not yet been passed, Stayton and his sup-

porters were sure it would be. They were right, and when Prohibition went into effect, Stayton and his organization worked to have the Eighteenth Amendment repealed. Most people thought that a repeal would be an impossible accomplishment. The skepticism of the American public was reflected in a Texas senator's statement: "There is as much chance of repealing the 18th Amendment as there is for a hummingbird to fly to Mars with the Washington Monument tied to its tail."

Stayton recruited wealthy and influential business leaders disillusioned with the effects of Prohibition into the AAPA, and

William Stayton founded the AAPA and encouraged the nation's most influential leaders to join.

by the end of the 1920s, the national directors of the AAPA included more than two hundred of the most powerful men in the nation. Stayton and his organization supported any political candidates who opposed Prohibition and worked to educate Americans about Prohibition's ill effects, such as the increase in crime and the loss of an estimated half-billion dollars a year in liquor tax.

Stayton particularly disliked the fact that Prohibition gave the federal government power to regulate behavior. In a speech at New York's Carnegie Hall, he said: "This prohibition business is only a symptom of a disease, the desire of fanatics to meddle in the other man's affairs and to regulate the details of your lives and mine."

After Stayton and the AAPA assisted in the successful repeal of the Eighteenth Amendment, they maintained a small Washington office under Stayton's direction to advise states on liquor control.

Franklin D. Roosevelt was born in 1882 in Hyde Park, New York. In 1932, he campaigned for the presidency. Aware of the public's growing support for a repeal of the Eighteenth Amendment, Roosevelt announced his support for a repeal. He also promised a tax on beer that would increase federal revenues by several hundred million dollars.

Roosevelt defeated the incumbent, Prohibition advocate Herbert Hoover, by a large margin. Immediately, his supporters began to work on an end to Prohibition. In the meantime, Roosevelt reduced the funds for the Prohibition Bureau and asked Congress to modify the Volstead Act to allow the legalization of beer. Seven days later, a bill was passed that redefined intoxicating liquor as above 3.2 percent alcohol. This made beer legal, and the public was jubilant.

Less than nine months later, the Eighteenth Amendment was repealed. Prohibition was finally over. Roosevelt stated, "I ask the wholehearted cooperation of all our citizens to the end that this return of individual freedom shall not be accompanied by the repugnant conditions that obtained prior to the adoption of the 18th amendment and those that have existed since its adoption."

Roosevelt was elected to four terms and served a total of twelve years before he died at the age of sixty-three from a cerebral hemorrhage.

Opposite: President Franklin D. Roosevelt opposed Prohibition. Above: Americans responded with elation when, just nine months after Roosevelt took office, the Eighteenth Amendment was repealed.

1785	Benjamin Rush suggests in his publication, *An Inquiry into the Effects of Ardent Spirits Upon the Human Body and Mind*, that alcohol consumption is detrimental to health.
1826	Lyman Beecher's sermons about temperance are published in a book titled *Six Sermons on the Nature, Occasions, Signs, Evils and Remedy of Intemperance*.
1869	The Prohibition Party is founded.
1874	The Women's Christian Temperance Union (WCTU) is formed.
1879	Frances Willard is elected national president of the WCTU.
1893	The Anti-Saloon League is founded.
1918	The Association Against the Prohibition Amendment is founded.
1919	The Eighteenth Amendment is ratified in January. Congress passes the Volstead Act in October.
1920	Prohibition officially begins in January.
1928	Eliot Ness is hired; his unit becomes known as the Untouchables.
1933	The Eighteenth Amendment is repealed and the Twenty-first Amendment is ratified.

By 1933, alcohol was no longer an illegal substance. Prohibition had run its course.

FOR FURTHER INFORMATION

BOOKS

Suzanne Lieurance, *The Prohibition Era in American History*. Berkeley Heights, NJ: Enslow, 2003.

Eileen Lucas, *The Eighteenth and Twenty-First Amendments*. Berkeley Heights, NJ: Enslow, 1998.

Dennis Nishi, *History Firsthand: Prohibition*. San Diego: Greenhaven, 2002.

Rebman Renee, *World History: Prohibition*. San Diego: Lucent, 1999.

WEBSITES

PBS
www.pbs.org
A biography of Al Capone and an overview of Prohibition can be found at the Public Broadcasting System's website.

University of Richmond
http://oncampus.richmond.edu
This website offers an interactive sixth-grade lesson plan on Prohibition.

About The Author

Tamra B. Orr is a full-time freelance writer and author. She has written more than two dozen nonfiction books for children and families, including *Fire Ants*, *The Journey of Lewis and Clark*, *The Biography of Astronaut Alan Shepard* and *The Parent's Guide to Homeschooling*. Orr attended Ball State University and received a B.S. degree in secondary education and English in 1982. Orr lives in Portland, Oregon, with her husband and four children, who range in age from seven to seventeen. She enjoys her job as an author because it teaches her something new every day.